# The Unfinished Work Week

## LOST PERSONAL TIME

### ANDREW GATERIEWICTZ

Printed by CreateSpace, an Amazon.com Company.

ISBN: 1475124236
ISBN 13: 9781475124231

Library of Congress Control Number: 2012905926
CreateSpace, North Charleston, SC

Thierry Breten CEO of ATOS, a French information technology company with 80,000 employees in 42 countries, stated, "We are producing data on a massive scale that is fast polluting our working environments and also encroaching into our personal lives."(1)

# DEDICATION

*This manuscript is a reality because of the influence, encouragement and open-mindedness of the people listed below. Without their successful implementation of new, unique philosophies in both their personal and business lives, these cutting edge strategies would never have been proven to minimize The Unfinished Work Week: Lost Personal Time.*

*A most sincere thank you to:*

| | |
|---|---|
| *Andrew Gateriewictz* | *Krystyna Gateriewictz* |
| *Ralph Cosenza* | *Sharee Chapman* |
| *Barbara Wierzbicki* | *Lisa Shasteen* |
| *Andrea O'Toole* | *Therese Flaherty* |
| *Phil Jaurigue* | *Trina Doussan* |
| *Elisa Coon* | *Kent Adams* |

# TABLE OF CONTENTS

................................................................

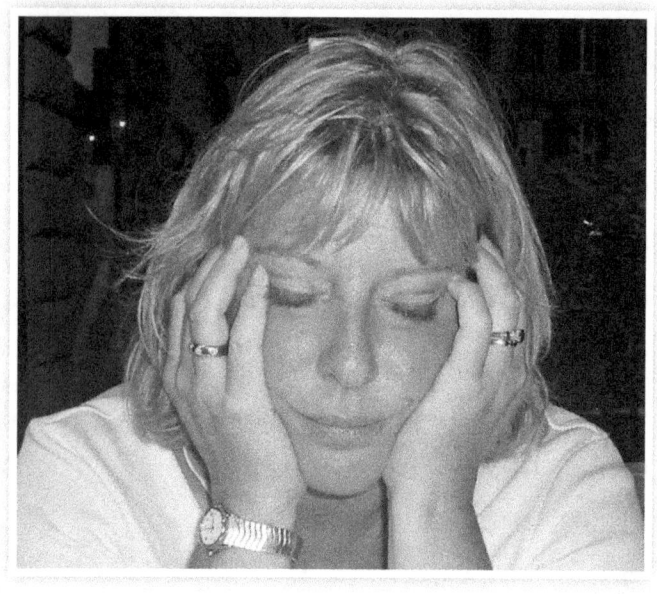

Fig. 1A

........................................................................

# THE UNFINISHED WORK WEEK: LOST PERSONAL TIME "THE 86% VISUAL SOLUTION"

If you are content with your current performance, as most average individuals are, then put this book down now!

Today's work environment has resulted in minimum head counts and larger workloads. Most of all, it has become expected for personal time on evenings and weekends be used to complete unfinished projects. The theory of do more with less has permeated throughout the corporate universe.

## This theory has its drawbacks.

In 2005 Microsoft Information Worker Product Management Group commissioned internationally respected productivity researcher, Dr. Larry Baker, to create a survey that helped participants assess their own productivity and receive tips on improving their work habits.(2) Listed below are the results of the survey which involved 38,000 workers in 200 countries.

1. 37% of the work week is unproductive or wasted
2. Unclear objectives
3. Lack of team communication
4. Ineffective meetings
5. Unclear priorities

Two areas in need of improvement stand out: 1) the amount of unproductive work time; and 2) the reasons for the non-productivity. Much of the wasted time necessitates extra interaction for the audience to remember the message originally presented. This repeated action costs companies thousands of dollars of employees' time. In order to eliminate the need for redundancy, a memorable conversation must be held. For this to happen, a person must understand how the memory works.

If one thinks giving information orally or written is easily retained by the recipient, consider the following list of facts. Each one is fighting for the attention of the audience, leaving little time for your message to be remembered.

Fact: The average number of corporate emails sent and received per person, per day is 115. (3)

Fact: Over 50% percent of a work day is spent managing email for the average corporate email user. (4)

Fact: 50% of the 30million PowerPoint Presentations given per day are considered a waste of time. (5)

Fact: The cost of poor PowerPoint Presentations is over $450,000 per day for a company with a minimum of 250 employees. (6)

Fact:    The brain has the capacity to remember only 8 new items of information in an hour. (7)

The events listed above cannot be eliminated. However, you can learn to use these tools more effectively by meeting one requirement: 86% of what is remembered is seen. (8)

*Effective visual interaction is the key to performance efficiencies and the ratio between working and personal time.*

What is available to reduce the strain and stress of everyday personal and business lives? Look no further than your laptop computer, desk top computer and smart cell phone. Technology has provided new ways to communicate in real time. Technology has changed the manner of communication from verbal to a visual-based process. Text messages, Emails and PowerPoint presentations have replaced phone calls and teleconferences.

Why would these companies abandon audible conversations at the expense of developing visual methods of communication?

They must know something.

*Communication efficiency is measured by what information is remembered during the first exposure.*

How is the Unfinished Work Week minimized? Combine the technological advances in communication methods with the rules of the visual memory process. Throughout the primary and secondary education processes, verbal communication was emphasized at the expense of visual interaction. So, now you can see the dilemma: in order to lower the non-productive work rate, you must learn how to have efficient and effective visual communication.

This journey will include the scientific reasons why visual, not verbal, communication is most effective. Then seven basic rules of effective conversation will be discussed and proven. Finally, we will use these rules in creating examples of memorable text messages, Emails, webinars, PowerPoint presentations, and face-to-face meetings, including SKYPE and ooVoo virtual conversations.

Adapting to emphasize visual rather than verbal conversation will not be an easy transition; simply because change in itself is difficult to accept. However, when a department's team commits and performs the new process, productivity will increase. Isn't it is time to use personal time to enjoy life rather than trying to catch up on unfinished work?

STOP!!! Take five minutes and identify how this new information can improve your personal and professional communication performance.

Fig: 2

......................................................................................

## CHAPTER ONE

# WHAT IS THE 86%
# VISUAL SOLUTION?

WARNING: You are about to be exposed to scientific facts that will improve the results of communicating with others. These facts will also prove that the communication process currently used by most business people, and taught by nationally known companies do not produce optimum results.

What is The 86% Visual Solution and how does it yield better communication results? It is the only method using the brain-controlled memory process in combination with visual communication to make the audience remember the key message. The spoken word is subservient to the non-spoken word.

Don't you agree this philosophy is different than the norm?

I, like everyone else, believed orally spoken questions, especially open-ended queries and answers, were the keys to successful negotiations. The open-ended questions were aimed to uncover the prospect's needs or pain or whatever "the word of the day" is. Once this information was verbally discovered, all that is left is to conduct a presentation addressing those needs or pains.

Was I shocked to discover something more important!!

Please keep a logical, open-mind as you learn new facts, and question yourself how this information affects your personal and department team's communication abilities and performance.

Since the main goal of communication is to have a conversation remembered, it is almost absurd to solely rely on the spoken word to achieve that goal. The brain doesn't like spoken words. There is too much work to decipher what is meant; especially in the English language. As an example, when the word "fine" is uttered, the brain has to perform the following activities:

1. Spell the word
2. Mentally "see" the spelled word
3. Interpret the meaning of the word
4. Decide to:
    a. Forget the word
    b. Use the word in short term working memory
    c. Enter the word into long term memory

That is a lot of work to do for just one spoken word. Now introduce the fact every person speaks an average of sixteen thousand words per day (9), and you begin to understand how easily our brain can become "overloaded." This results in some words being processed and others thrown by the wayside. The question should be, "which of my words are actually being remembered." Recalled conversations have a direct effect on both daily personal and work lives. Think about it, are your clients retaining the words you want remembered?

This is not the first time this question has been asked. For years, behavioral scientists have been conducting research to determine how the brain creates memories. Originally it was widely accepted verbal communication was most important. Then the Information Highway explosion occurred which included the development of super fast personal and commercial computers, as well as, other electronic devices. This new method of communication and the gathering of knowledge opened a universe of new theories which have uncovered facts that negate previous beliefs.

*Of course, one of these negated beliefs was that the memory was verbally controlled.* In 2003, a huge discovery was made with the use of an MRI. Scientists traced the flow of blood through the neurons of the brain after being both visually and verbally stimulated. The results proved, without any doubts, the brain-controlled memory process is dominated by sight . . . . not hearing. (10) The difference is not minimal; quite the opposite. Consider this fact, of what a person remembers 86% is seen . . . . only 9% heard.

Time to ask another question: "If it is known the brain is visually dominant, why do you continue to rely on speaking rather than sight to have the audience remember the key message?" This makes no sense.

Unlike the spoken word, the brain processes visual topics instantly. There is no need to spell the word because it is seen. There is no need to develop a picture because the picture is being seen. There is no need to interpret the vision, because the brain sees and hears the topic simultaneously. These facts effect the ability for an audience to remember the new information. Other methods to insure the key information is retained are:

1. Writing down information
2. Reading out loud
3. Listening
4. Seeing

Each helps to engage more than one sense at the same time. In other words, adding colorful charts, cartoons, diagrams to a text increases the memorization process. But, be sure to follow an important rule. All visual aids used in communication must support the important subject to be remembered. Be careful, just to use fun and colorful graphics to stimulate attention will not necessarily result in the audience obtaining your offered knowledge. Another question to ask is, "Am I using the visual aids at my disposal in the correct manner to attain optimum memory results?"

As you continue this journey of "The Unfinished Work Week: Lost Personal Time," there will be a quick quiz. The answers will form the basis of the "Memory Rules." A chapter will be devoted to each answer to describe its importance in delivering a memorable communication through text messaging, Email, video conferences, PowerPoint presentations and, most of all, face-to-face interaction. Practicing just one or a few of these rules will not have the desired impact. One must follow all seven rules to insure the key message is retained by the audience. Whether that audience is a peer, subordinate, student, client or board of directors . . . their memories are the keys to your success.

STOP!!! Take five minutes and identify how this new information can improve your personal and professional communication performance.

Fig: 3

.......................................................................

## CHAPTER TWO

# ATTENTION!! ATTENTION!!

All hands on deck!! It is time to discuss another activity that affects peoples' memory systems. No matter how accomplished a person becomes in the communication topics included in the coming chapters, creating a memorable message also depends on someone else. . . . the audience.

The audience must participate in the memory game in order for your message to be remembered. The audience may be difficult; difficult for the listeners that exhibit the attitude of indifference. You have seen it. They think no one has anything new to offer them. This leads to inattention. No matter what important new information presented, these people believe it is not needed in their life. These "indifferents" are the proverbial, "lead the horse to water, but you can't make them drink." So, as my friends from the Northeast say, "forget about 'em!!"

On the other hand, there are people believing your key message is newly founded and will improve their lives. They display an attitude of acceptance and will pay attention as long as the "performance lives up to its billing."

The key word here is attention. There are three types of attention which are present in any conversation. If you want the audience to remember the important information, it is a must to define the different types of attention.

Behavioral scientists have discovered there are three types of attention. These being (11):

- Controlled
- Stimuli
- Arousal

Believe me, all of us have not only seen these attention behaviors, but also have experienced them ourselves. Besides words and visual aids, many things can have a direct effect on a person's type of attention. Surely, you have attended the same event with a colleague in which you apply more attention to different topics than your colleague. And the opposite is also true.

A person's curiosity undoubtedly arouses the attention level. Not knowing what is "behind door #1" makes you want to go through the entrance. To create greater interest, you are made aware the item behind the door has value for you. Now you are cutting in front of people to be first to see the promised personal asset. Curiosity may arouse a person's attention, but what sustains the attention span?

In later chapters a discussion will center on the two factors of how to awaken and keep a person's attention. First, it is important to define each type of attention. Once this information is known, it will allow for personal interaction adjustments to produce desired results.

Fig: 4

## Controlled Attention:

A person forces themselves to concentrate on the subject at hand. When a person is in the state of controlled attention, they become unaware of their surroundings, both visual and auditory. It's like going into a trance. An example can be a student "cramming" the night before the big exam. Knowing they have to remember certain topics, they block everything else out so as not to be disturbed in the memorization process. All this is attributed to the concentration power of the brain. It is fascinating what this gray matter is capable of and how it reacts to "outside" influences. Remember, this is "control central" that directs a person's every human experience. The more you know the basic functions of the brain, the more effective your interaction skills become.

## Stimuli Attention:

This occurs when a person involuntarily is attracted to an unexpected event. In other words something happens to break the "spell" of controlled attention. It may be a ringing phone, someone spills a cup of coffee, or the noise

Fig: 5

of a message notification on your cell phone. Whatever the cause, you must concentrate to re-establish controlled attention to get the most from the memory process.

## Arousal Attention:

This is the state of mind when the attention span has reached its maximum or when the topic being discussed becomes monotonous and boring. At any rate, the brain has become tired of the same thing. To recapture the attention of the audience to controlled or stimuli attention you must inject some "caffeine" into the conversation to "arouse" the memory system to start working again.

Fig: 6

It is interesting to note, an adult attention span can actually last twenty minutes. Most of the time the person you are trying to "reach" wavers between controlled and stimuli attention. As stated earlier, your brain has a limited capacity to store memories. That capacity dictates to you, the presenter, to keep the discussion of any key message to a minimum of 8 to 10 minutes if you want it remembered.

For the time being, remember, if a person does not focus attention on something, they will not remember it!!

This fact leads to a couple of important questions:

- How do you attract someone's attention visually and verbally?
- How do you maintain someone's attention visually and verbally?

Discovering the answers to these questions is the first step in minimizing The Unfinished Work Week.

STOP!!! Take five minutes and identify how this new information can improve your personal and professional communication performance.

Fig: 7

....................................................................

## CHAPTER THREE

# THE 86% VISUAL
# SOLUTION QUIZ

As stated at the beginning of the book, "If you are content with your current performance, as most average individuals are, then put the book down now. Continue if you understand the current process always has area for improvement. This improvement allows you to surpass your company's expectations."

Now is the time to prove why a person needs to improve their professional communication results. Whether you are a teacher, manager, sales person or CEO addressing an audience, the main goal is to have the key message retained. In order for that to happen, one has to follow the "rules of the brain-controlled memory." Let's find out how much you know about the basic memory facts. As the quick quiz is completed, after each question ask yourself, "How does this fact affect my performance?"

This exercise will also prove why changing from verbal to visual-based communication is a necessity.

Take as long as you want to complete the quiz. There is no time limit, so let's start now.

Fig: 8

1. What percent of an 8 hour day's events are forgotten?

Fig: 8

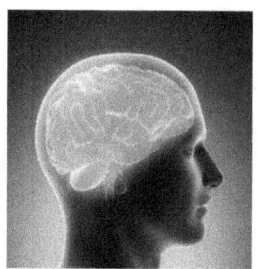

Fig: 9

2. What are the 2 keys to unlock the brain-controlled memory?

**Fig: 10**

3. How many new items of information can the brain remember in 1 hour?

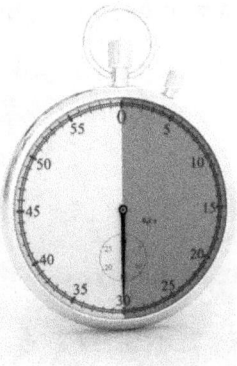

**Fig: 11**

4. Verbal short term memory can process how many items of data heard in 30 seconds?

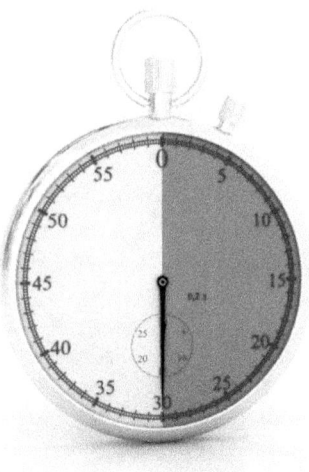

Fig: 12

5. Visual short term memory can process how many items of data seen in 30 seconds?

Fig: 13

6. What percent of face-to-face conversation is non-verbal?

Fig: 14

7. Of what you remember, what percent is seen?

Now for the answers and how they have a direct influence on how efficiently and effectively business interaction is conducted. The purpose of this little quiz is not to highlight what you do not know about the brain-controlled memory process. Instead, it is the initial exposure to the qualifications needed to have your key message remembered. As is asked at the end of each segment of this book, take five minutes to understand how each answer affects the results of your business communication.

**Fig: 15**

1. What percent of an 8 hour day's events are forgotten? Believe it or not 90% of the activities in 8 hours are forgotten! (12) What a huge number. Think of what this fact means. If you see someone at 9:00 A.M., what are the chances that person will remember the conversation by 5:00 P.M.? This is just another reason why it is imperative for a business person to learn how to make the audience remember what should be remembered. Once the "Memory Rules" are learned and used, your important message will be retained all day. This is a distinct advantage over the competition. Let those people continue to use the same old communication techniques that result in little recall by the client. What a great feeling, knowing your discussion will be remembered at the conclusion of the client's daily schedule.

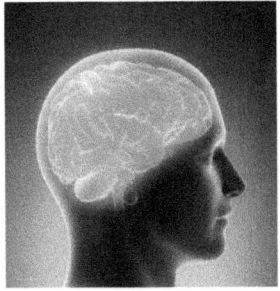

Fig: 16                              Fig: 17

2.  What are the 2 keys to unlock the brain-controlled memory?

Personal and Meaningful Information (13)

Ever wonder why you may remember some topics and easily forget others when participating in a meeting? What keys unlock the door to the brain's memory banks? Just two types of words open the brain to processing new ideas: personal and meaningful. It has been proven the brain-controlled memory does not entertain every word or conversation. So, many of the 16,000 words per day a person utters never gets processed. Instead, the majority gets cast aside without even a mental "look see." Isn't it nice to know most of what is said never even gets heard?

8

Fig: 18

3. How many new items of information can the brain remember in 1 hour?

Even though computers were modeled after the human brain; the human brain cannot compare with the analytical power of these technological devices. A computer can immediately remember data as fast as you type and hit the save button. Unlike the computer, our brains only have the capacity to remember 8 new items of data in 1 hour, and it takes 8 seconds to transfer information from short term working memory through the brain's hippocampus to long term memory.(13)

How many new ideas did you introduce during your last 1 hour meeting? How many of those new ideas were remembered by the audience?

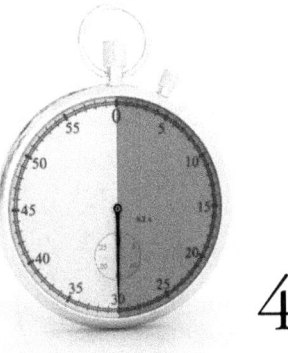

4

Fig: 19

4. Verbal short term memory can process how many items of data heard in 30 seconds?

This answer once was the behavioral scientist Miller's Magic Number of 7. However, this study was performed before the age of:

    a. Computers
    b. Email
    c. Instant messaging
    d. Open work cubicles

With these examples of the different situations competing for our attention, the Magic Number 7 has decreased to the Magic Number of 4 verbal topics being processed in 30 seconds. (14)

15

Fig: 20

5.  Visual short term memory can process how many items of data seen in 30 seconds?

The difference between the processing of verbal versus visual items is gigantic. If this answer doesn't make you change the emphasis from hearing to seeing communication, then nothing else will. Visual short term memory can process up to 15 visual bits of data in 30 seconds. PLUS, the visual short term memory lasts at least 4 times longer than verbal!! (15)

66%

Fig: 21

6.  What percent of face-to-face conversation is non-verbal?

It seems strange to me the educational system goes to great lengths to teach students everything about the English language. A student gets familiar with nouns, pronouns, adjectives, verbs and adverbs. Once comfortable with these aspects of the language, you can then proceed to create sentences in order to communicate with others. This all seems strange to me because only 33% of face to face conversation is verbal. That's right! The unspoken word accounts for the majority of the communication . . . a whopping 66%!!! (16)

Question: How much time is given a student by the educational system to teach unspoken dialogue?

Answer: None.

Fact: the body exposes over 54,000 different phrases and/or sentences. How many of these different phrases and sentences do you understand?

86%

Fig: 22

7. Of what you remember, what percent is seen?

Hint: the answer was given in an earlier chapter. So, in case you have forgotten, the answer is 86%. Yes, 86% of what a person remembers is seen and only 9% heard. This fact is the cornerstone of The 86% Visual Solution.

You will be reminded of these answers at the end of each of the following chapters. These seven facts form the litmus test for memorable conversation. Reminder: A litmus test is a crucial and revealing test in which there is one decisive factor.

90% - P & M - 8:1 - 4:30 - 15:30 - 66% - 86%

STOP!!! Take five minutes and identify how this new information can improve your personal and professional communication performance.

90%

Fig: 23

# CHAPTER FOUR

..................................................................

# 90%

As mentioned earlier, the goal of communication is to be remembered.

What are the chances your message will be remembered by the audience at the end of the day? The first question of the Memory Quiz introduced the unbelievable answer. The memory has the capacity to recall only 10% of the events in an 8 hour work day!!

Jenkins and Dallenback's Learning Curve shows that in five minutes, much of the information we have taken in is lost. After an hour - two thirds of it is lost. And after a day has passed - 90 % of it is lost.(17) This really is the curve of forgetting. Did you realize the average memory operates at such a low retention rate? Surprising, isn't it. The question becomes, "Why?" Realize it is not all your fault. If a person is espousing too much information at one time, the memory system has to be selective to the words chosen to be processed.

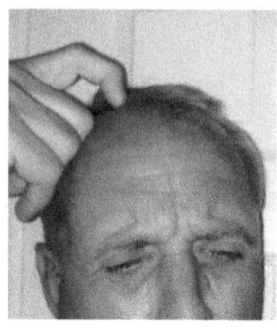

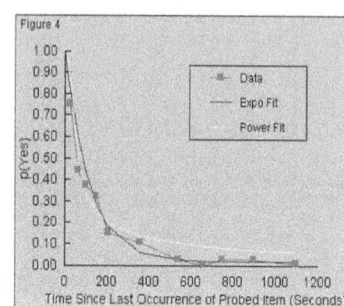

Fig: 24                    Fig: 25

Why do we talk about the 90% forget rate in the beginning? Because we should know the obstacles to improving The Unfinished Work Week.

- What is the plan to overcome these memory roadblocks?
- What must be adjusted to create more effective interaction with our peers, clients, subordinates or stakeholders?
- What does it take to get included in that 10% retention pool?

The first step is to realize we talk too much. You know it and I know it. Never mind trying to have the audience remember what you have said. My question is, "How much do you remember what you said during the business day?" Listed below are four quotes by well known people regarding the "gift of gab." These statements may be fun to read, but the message is very serious regarding verbal based conversation.

"The way to get started is to quit talking and begin doing."

Walt Disney

"It was impossible to get a conversation going; everybody was talking too much."

Yogi Berra

"It's no use of talking unless people understand what you say."

Zora Neale Hurston

"The most important thing with communication is to hear what is not being said."

Anonymous

What message is being related? There are a lot of non-essential words uttered during the day. What has to be done is limit these words when holding business conversations. The result of all these needless verbal expressions is "word overload" which is not conducive to improving The Unfinished Work Week . . . . . quite the opposite.

90% - P & M - 8:1 - 4:30 - 15:30 - 66% - 86%

STOP!!! Take five minutes and identify how this new information can improve your personal and professional communication performance.

Fig: 26

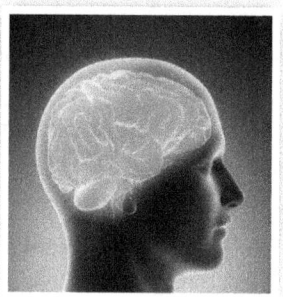

Fig: 27

**CHAPTER FIVE**

·····················································

# PERSONAL AND MEANINGFUL

Author Franklin P. Jones (1908-1980) coined the following true yet comical phrase, "one advantage of talking to yourself, is that at least you know someone is listening."(18)

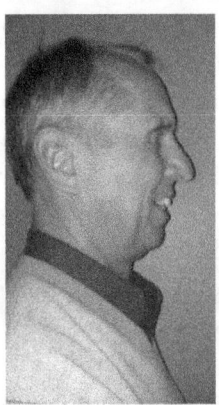

Fig: 28

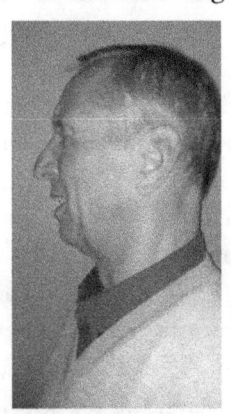

Fig: 29

We begin the "Memory Rules" with the second most important answer in the quiz. Why? Two reasons; first, without knowing and understanding the keys to open the door to the brain so information can be processed, we will never approach working memory.(19) The second reason is the second most important items in a list are always presented at the beginning. The most important topic is mentioned last. This is the order the brain absorbs information. So, remember that little tidbit of information the next time you create an agenda for a meeting or presentation.

Mr. Franklin P. Jones probably never knew the reason why his statement was truthful. But he did realize most conversations were forgotten. Probably, even his own.

When a person is a child most everything is personal and meaningful because the world is a fascinating place of activity. From childhood we learn new things to please, not just ourselves, but also those around us, including family and friends. As we get older, this "personal and meaningful key" takes on another proportion, which is the need to succeed. Peer pressure is introduced into our lives. No one wants to be 200$^{th}$ out of a class of 200 students. Some type of extra-curriculum activity such as drama clubs, chorus, band or sports enters the personal scene. You join these activities because of the "keys": personal and meaningful reasons. Certain skills are learned to succeed in your chosen professional career. The need to excel to make an income to support our family's anticipated and wanted lifestyle. If that is not a personal and meaningful reason to further one's education, than I do not understand the "keys"!!!

But for some reason most of adult working people stop searching for education to improve their performance. Some employees are forced to expand knowledge because their industries demand Continuing Education Units (CEU) to maintain a certain certification. Prime examples of these industries are education, real estate and technology.

Question: what about the largest occupations that effect the efficient operation of companies? Why aren't sales people, managers, investment bankers and even CEOs forced to take new, unique courses to improve their communication skills? As leaders of other employees and trustees of others' investments, it would be thought they would always be searching for new, more efficient and productive ways to enhance performance.

The answer is complacency. The great business mastermind, Jack Welch addressed the attitude of complacency in this fashion, "The mind-set of yesterday's manager—accepting compromise, keeping things tidy . . . breeds complacency. Today's leaders must rally around a vision of what an organization can become." Organizations must always strive to get better and faster... or get beaten! We knew every process could be improved and productivity increased. I urged every employee to accept and embrace change and to see change for the growth opportunities it brings."[20]

Complacency allows others to pass you. Complacency leads to being 200th out of a class of 200. Complacency stops using the creative powers of the brain-controlled memory. Complacency leads to a dull and boring life. No wonder most people believe work is a four letter word like "toil." That feeling of work has helped a national restaurant chain succeed. What eatery is that? TGIF . . . Thank Goodness It's Friday. Dull and boring complacency has also led to the expression of "Hump Day" as a replacement for Wednesday. Isn't it a good feeling to think, unlike your peers, that work is a three letter word called fun? The workplace is always full of new personal and meaningful areas of knowledge waiting to be explored. Waiting for you to increase your performance in order to attain and maintain that expected lifestyle for your family.

So, now the biggest obstacle for the "personal and meaningful keys" to open the memory door has been identified . . . the word is complacency. How is this barrier overcome in order to have a chance the important information will be remembered by the audience? You must learn a new way for this information to become personal and meaningful to your client. The subject must become important enough for the brain to open its door.

Hint: Because the long term memory is biased toward phrases remembered in the past, you cannot open a conversation with any phrase which led to a negative result. (21) The brain remembers this phrase and automatically tells the memory not to process any other information. You have undoubtedly heard the expression, "I've heard that before," even before you completed your verbal thought.

Now it is time for some needed definitions.

- First, what is a Key Topic? A Key Topic is the main knowledge you want the audience to remember.
- Second, what makes a Key Topic meaningful? A meaningful Key Topic is full of significance, purpose, and value.
- Third, what makes a Key Topic personal? A personal Key Topic relates to an individual or an individual's character, conduct, motives or private affairs.
- Fourth, what makes a Key Topic personal and meaningful? A personal and meaningful Key Topic is significant information which positively affects an individual's motives as it pertains to performance.

The last definition is a result of a logical progression based on facts. The first step in communication is to identify the Key Topics that must be remembered. Since personal and meaningful are intangible emotions, the Key Topic must be introduced not with a product or service. Instead, the introduction to the brain-controlled memory must be what the positive effect the product or service has on the individual.

Think of a Key Topic as key words a computer recognizes in a search. If you have a web site, the site is assigned to key words which a researcher enters into the search box. Only problem is that yours is not the only homepage that will appear in the inquiry. Because there is a limit for the number of key words, web sites get batched into categories which can create a rather large universe of companies similar to yours. To be noticed and remembered in a computer search, the topic has to be different. Personal and meaningful are the keys.

Like the search engine of a computer, the client must be offered those unique, different key words that will entice the brain to "click on" your Key Topic web site. So what are these personal and meaningful keys? You have to have both . . . having one will not open the combination lock to memory. Remember the definition of a Key Topic: "*significant* information which positively affects an individual's *motives* as it pertains to *performance*." Three key words stand out: *significant, motives and performance*. It is your responsibility to create phrases that fall into the category of each key word. Identifying the meaning of the words is simple and most important. Significant means important information the audience does not know. Motive is the reason the client will undertake a task. And, performance results in winning, losing or somewhere in between.

Now that you understand what Key Topics are, complete a list of key words under each Key Topic that will open the doors to the brains of your audience. Whether it be a prospective account, seasoned salespeople, C-level managers or an IPO startup company, each will entertain a discussion with you if the topic is personal and meaningful.

90% - P & M - 8:1 - 4:30 - 15:30 - 66% - 86%

STOP!!! Take five minutes and identify how this new information can improve your personal and professional communication performance.

8

Fig: 30

........................................................................

## CHAPTER SIX

# 8 : 1

Now comes a rather shocking fact included in the Memory Rules book. Some very important communication facts have been uncovered that will alter the way Key Topics are retained. Now is the time for a quick review of these items.

- The keys to open the brain's door to ignite the memory process are meaningful (significant) and personal (motive) topics.
- The brain can only process 4 verbal items of information in 30 seconds.
- The mind can process 15 visual situations in 30 seconds; outperforming verbal more than 3 times!!
- Short-Term Visual Memory also last 4 times longer than Short-Term Verbal Memory!!
- If the Key Topic is to be remembered, the type of communication must be changed from verbal to visual. Words have to support sight. Remember, "eyes remember better than ears"!!!

- The transition from verbal-based to visual-based discussions already exists, because 66% of any face-to-face conversation is silent communication. This is the language of the body. That only takes learning some of the 54,000 different phrases and sentences not spoken.
- By self-diagnosis, it has been discovered sight-based communication will improve your personal and professional communication performance.
- The audience can remember what you want them to remember.

Hopefully you have learned, discussed, practiced and used all this new information. The transformation from verbal to vision dominated communication has been accomplished!! So just what reward is achieved? You were warned about the shocking fact. Now is the time to divulge the great reward. The brain has the capacity to remember ONLY 8 new items of information in one hour!! That is what 8:1 means.

In order to better understand this fact, the brain-controlled memory process must be reviewed. If the goal is to have the audience remember what you want them to remember, then the path to Working and Long-Term Memory must be followed. Think of the stops on this path as elimination checkpoints. We already know the brain only has the capacity to remember 8 new items in an hour. The number that will be retained will be less as no machine, including the brain, can operate at 100% capacity all the time. A large part of the reason the number is less than eight, is you are not using visual communication correctly to increase the probability the Key Topic will be accepted by Working or Long-Term Memory. So what are these elimination checkpoints? I will explain them in non-scientific terms.

## *Checkpoint #1*

Sensory Memory: The Sensory Memory retains an exact copy of what is seen or heard. It only lasts for a few seconds. In fact, some theorize it last only 300 milliseconds. It has unlimited capacity.(22)

## *Checkpoint #2*

Verbal Short-Term Memory (VSTM): Selective attention to personal and meaningful information determines what data moves from Sensory Memory to Short-Term Memory. It works basically the same as a computer's RAM (Random Access Memory) in that it provides a working space for short computations and then transfers it to other parts of the memory system or discards it. Verbal Short-Term Memory is vulnerable to interruption or interference.(23)

## *Checkpoint #3*

Visual Short-Term Memory (VSTM): is a type of short-term memory, and one limited to information within the visual domain. Unlike Verbal Short-Term memory, Visual Short- Term Memory is not fragile, doesn't decay or forgets rapidly. VSTM is capable of being actively maintained. Visual Short-Term Memories are robust to subsequent visions and last over many seconds.(24)

## *Checkpoint #4*

Recently a new form of visual memory, similar to a holding tank, has been identified that is between Sensory Memory and Visual Short-Term Memory. This holding tank has high capacity (up to 15 items) and prolonged memory duration time (up to 4 times that of verbal).(25)

## *Checkpoint #5*

Verbal-Working Memory: You have now entered the most important step of the memory process. Your personal and meaningful message making it this far means one thing, the Key Topic has a better chance it will be one of the 8 new bits of information remembered by the audience in one hour. The chances can be improved to 100% by using the biggest rule of Working Memory . . . rehearsal. The Working Memory enriches both Verbal and Visual Memory topics. Verbal information is stored and prevents forgetting by continuously articulating its contents, thereby refreshing the information in a rehearsal loop. As an example: think of how many old phone numbers you remember and those you only knew for a period of time.(26)

## *Checkpoint #6*

Visual-Working Memory: The Visual-Working Memory has a visuo-spatial sketch pad (VSSP), which stores visual and spatial information. Spatial information describes the physical location of objects and the relationship between objects. It can be used for constructing and manipulating visual images, and for the representation of mental maps. The Visual-Working Memory is responsible for directing attention to relevant information. Also, it coordinates dual tasking, by acting in conjunction with Verbal-Working Memory.(27)

*Checkpoint* #7

Long-Term Memory (LTM): The knowledge we store in Long-Term Memory affects perceptions of the world, and influences what information in the environment will be processed. Long-Term Memory provides the framework to which new knowledge is attached. It contrasts with Short-Term and Working Memory in that information can be stored for extended periods of time and the limits of its capacity are not known.(28) This is the optimum landing space for a Key Topic. The audience remembers the Key Topic for an unspecified amount of time. Accomplishing this task means someone has lost a space in your client's memory to you. One competitor was just eliminated!!

Congratulations, you just won round one!! Now the same process has to be followed to have all of the Key Topics retained by the client. The audience now remembers what you wanted them to remember.

90% - P & M - 8:1 - 4:30 - 15:30 - 66% - 86%

STOP!!! Take five minutes and identify how this new information can improve your personal and professional communication performance.

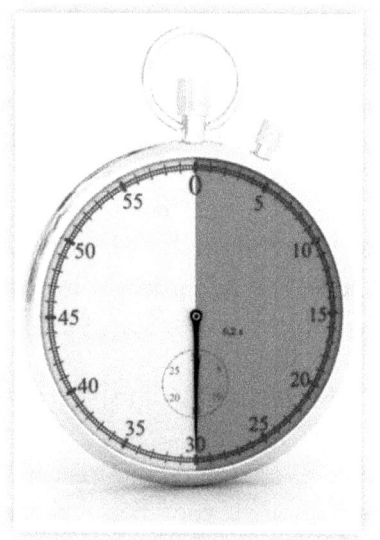

4

Fig: 31

....................................................................

## CHAPTER SEVEN

# 4:30

After using the personal and meaningful keys to unlock the brain's door, it is time to take the opportunity to engage the audience in a discussion. In order to have the person remember what you want them to remember, the expression 4:30 must be adhered to. No, 4:30 is not an important time. But it is an important number. Remember? Verbal-Short Term Memory can process how many items of data heard in 30 seconds? The answer was 4 audio topics can be processed in 30 seconds.

It is important to understand in the past the average was 7 verbal bits of information could be processed in 30 seconds. This was discovered by George Miller's classic 1956 study that found the amount of information which can be remembered in one exposure is between five and nine items, depending on the information. Applying a range of +2 or -2, the number 7 became known as *Miller's Magic Number*, the number of items which can be held in Short-Term Memory at any one time.

Miller himself stated that his magic number was for items with one aspect. His work was based on subjects listening to a number of auditory tones that varied only in pitch. Each tone was presented separately, and the subject was asked to identify each tone relative to the others they had already heard, by assigning it a number. After about five or six tones, subjects began to get confused, and their capacity for making further tone judgments broke down.

Rather a controlled environment to hang your hat on. Never mind stating how the mind operates in processing information that actually gets by the front door. Over the years, human behavioral scientists have re-visited George Miller's work and enlarged the scope of the experiment to include today's average work environment. As mentioned previously, the tests were conducted with:

- Computers running with multiple windows opened
- Incoming and outgoing Email with sound notifications
- Cell phones ringing
- Multi-tasking
- Ceiling-less offices or cubicles

The results of conducting Miller's experiment in today's ultra-technological world are most disappointing. The Miller Magic Number 7 has decreased to the Magic Number of 4 audible topics that can be processed in 30 seconds.

Just what is the "processing of information" and why is it significant to our motives for performing? When information enters into our mind, our brain has to make some instant decisions. These decisions include:

1. Do not allow the information to enter the Short-Term Memory "holding cell."
2. Allow the information to enter the "holding cell" and determine its fate within 30 seconds.
3. The information will be used in Short-Term Working Memory.
4. The information is most personal and meaningful and will be transferred to Long-Term Memory.

Remember, the goal is to have the audience remember what you want remembered. So, of course, the Key Topic has to be included in the transfer to Working and Long-Term Memory. How is this accomplished?

Think of the processing of 4 items of new information in 30 seconds as an empty 4 ounce glass bowl ready to be filled with M&M's peanut candies. Your favorites are the brown M&M's. You carefully start filling the bowl ensuring the favorites are the greatest in number. But as the bag begins to empty, a mad rush of M&M's suddenly pours into the bowl causing the candies to overflow. Included in the discarded candies are some of those delicious brown M&M's. The 4 ounce bowl has kept some candies you don't like in 30 seconds.

Now apply this appetizing example to verbal conversation. Knowing the mind can only handle 4 new audio ideas in 30 seconds, it is imperative to choose those four topics carefully. Those four ideas can be reiterated within the 30 second span and not overflow the brain's capacity to process the selected information. Also, these four pieces of information offered in 30 seconds should support one of your Key Topics. Different than you are used to, isn't it? Slow yourself down and adhere to the 4:30 rule. Or is it preferred to continue the current verbal onslaught during discussions and get the same results?  Ever hear the audience say, "I don't recall you saying that?"  Do you want to continue hearing that?  Isn't it the goal to have the Key Topic remembered?  A reminder, the current definition of insanity is doing the same thing over and over again expecting a different result.  I guess the real question becomes, "How much longer do you want to be recognized as being insane?"

90% - P & M - 8:1 - 4:30 - 15:30 - 66% - 86%

STOP!!! Take five minutes and identify how this new information can improve your personal and professional communication performance.

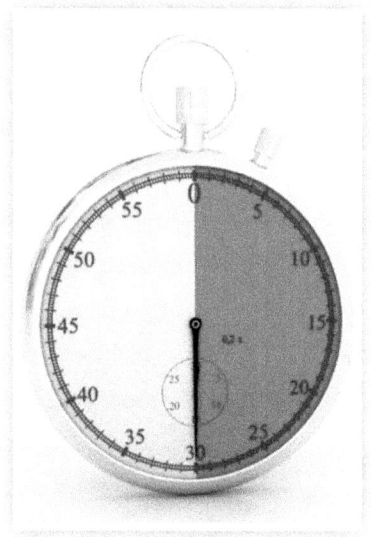

15

Fig: 32

..........................................................................

## CHAPTER EIGHT

15:30

Just like Chapter Seven, we begin with a number that looks like the time. But it actually answers the question, how many items of data seen in 30 seconds can Visual-Short Term Memory process? In case you have forgotten, the answer is Visual-Short Term Memory can process up to 15 visual items of data in 30 seconds. PLUS, the Visual-Short Term Memory lasts at least 4 times longer than verbal!! So the comparison between Verbal and Visual-Short term Memory is 4:30 versus 15:30. The difference is gigantic. If this answer doesn't make a person change communication emphasis from hearing to seeing than nothing else will!!

Take a look at some visual versus verbal facts to explain why the processing capacity is extremely different. Don't start thinking a scientific exploration is about to begin, because only three results are being considered:

- Verbal-Short Term Memory is an example of how the brain processes information differently when it is received through hearing or seeing. The auditory procedure is very different from the visual process. To begin the process, the brain must first hear spoken words. This is a difficult task, as the brain is required to create images from spoken words. When an item is presented through auditory communication, the Verbal-Short Term Memory must perform more than one function to interpret the message.

- Visual-Short Term Memory has a longer and more accurate duration than auditory Short-Term Memory, because the item being presented is remembered by two different brain functions within Short-Term Memory. The item processed visually is digested by a visual receiver within the brain. For example, the visual information is seen and heard through rehearsal maintenance in the brain at the same time. This is the basis for the expression, "Key Topic: See. Discuss. Remember."

- Visual-Short Term Memory also has an intermediate visual storage area. This "Holding Tank" holds a high capacity of visual information (up to 15 items); and prolonged memory duration much longer than Verbal Short Term Memory. This high capacity visual "Holding Tank" seems to exist for at least four seconds longer than verbal.

Isn't the human brain something else? A person always thinks they are in control of activities, when, in fact, the brain does as it pleases. In fact, the brain controls and directs your activities. Especially those actions you are not aware are being done.

Now you have found out, without any doubt, the spoken word has far, far less impact on your client's memory than visual communication.

Does this mean you should only use of sign language in all conversations?  Heavens no!!

Does it mean to adjust the presentation process to emphasize visual components rather than verbal? Yes.

Does it mean using the spoken 4:30 ratio in support of the sight's 15:30 ratio?  Yes.

Does it mean the need to change the manner of communication to insure the Key Topics will be remembered? Yes.

A sample of some of the common visual tools used to support and express the Key Topic are:

1.  The Written Word/Email/Text Messaging
    A person reading a personal and meaningful document will have a far greater probability of retaining the information.  Use key words to support the Key Topics in an agenda, supporting documents and notes from previous meetings.  Remember the 4:30 rule and keep the messages brief.

2.  Flipcharts/White Boards
    These can be used to write down key points during the discussion or they can be prepared and used during the presentation.  Use several different colored pens to highlight key points.

3.  Laptop with LCD Projector
    These are most popular and reliable. Using a program such as Microsoft PowerPoint, a presentation can be designed on a computer that can then be

displayed on an LCD projector. As a precaution, it is best to copy the presentation on a flash drive in case of total equipment failure.

4. Props

These are everyday objects that can be used as visual aids to enhance the discussion. To ensure the attendees can see the objects, the props should be objects that can be passed around the audience.

5. Sketches/Role Play

These are small presentations that simulate a point or part of your presentation. Role plays are a most powerful way to "prove" the Key Topics credibility.

6. Webinars/Video Conferencing/SKYPE/ooVoo

Have you noticed the increasing use of technological visual communication? First, the telecommunications industry went away from telephone conference calls to video conferencing. Then larger Fortune 500 companies followed. And now any size company can hold a visual meeting. Why the change from hearing to seeing? The answer is simple. Eyes remember better than ears. The result is more effective and efficient meetings without unnecessary travel.

7. The Human Body

A full chapter in this book is devoted to non-verbal communication through the human body's movements of postures, positions, gestures and distances. This subject is so important because it represents 66% of face –to-face communication.

So tell me, are you sane or insane? Are you going to continue to rely on speaking to have the Key Topic remembered? Or finally do the intelligent thing? The answer should be yes. Change and finally accept the fact the audience has to see the Key Topic in order for it to be remembered.

90% - P & M - 8:1 - 4:30 - 15:30 - 66% - 86%

STOP!!! Take five minutes and identify how this new information can improve your personal and professional communication performance.

66%

Fig: 33

## CHAPTER NINE

................................................................

## *66%*

As that great philosopher Robert McCloskey once said, "I know you believe you understand what you think I said . . . . but I am not sure you realize that what you heard, is not what I meant."(29)

Even Mr. McCloskey knew eyes remember better than ears. Which leads to the question, "How in the world am I going to change communicating from speaking to showing?"

Well, the answer is 66% of any face-to-face conversation is non-verbal. Nothing has to change except a little education. Intuitively you already sense or feel what the other person is silently saying. Also realize the audience is also sensing or feeling the same way about your actions. Silent conversation conveys interpersonal information and has 5 times the impact of verbal communication.(30) Once again the brain's memory door is easily opened by sight . . . . the sight of watching bodies talk to one another.

As with most of the subjects of these chapters, an entire book could be written just for this particular topic. This topic, silent communication, contains over 54,000 different phrases and sentences. It is impossible to cover the entire language here. However, some of the basic foundations can be introduced that make up this form of communication. Like its counterpart, verbal speaking, the non-verbal language also has nouns, verbs, adjectives and adverbs. They are in the form of a person's positions, postures, gestures and distances. And like the spoken word, in order to form a complete phrase or sentence, the positions, postures, gestures and distances all have to be "read" at one time. If the actions are not observed at the same time, again like the spoken word, the meaning will be taken out of context. In other words, a false conclusion will be formed due to a misread interpretation.

As mentioned above, first the nouns, verbs, adjectives and adverbs must be identified. These are in the form of positions, postures, gestures and distances.

**Positions:** Where a person places themselves in relation to other people or objects.

Examples:

1. Standing next to someone facing forward
2. Standing slightly behind someone
3. Sitting directly across from someone
4. Standing or sitting behind a desk

**Postures**: How a person positions the limbs (arms and legs) and the whole body to create an attitude.

Examples:

1. Sitting with arms and legs crossed

2. Standing and leaning against a door way
3. Sitting with legs on desk and arms behind head
4. Standing facing a person with legs apart and hands on hips

**Gestures**: The movement of part of the body, especially hands, legs or the head, to express a specific message. Examples:

1. Raised eyebrows with squinted eyes
2. Hands to the mouth, eyes or ears
3. Handshake with the palm up
4. Seated with leg crossed pointed at the person seated next to you

**Distances**: The space around your body that you invite people to enter.

1. Intimate Zone: 0-18 inches
2. Personal Zone: 18 inches to 4 feet
3. Social Zone: 4 feet to 12 feet
4. Public Zone: 12 feet and over

It cannot be said enough times, remember, interpret each component at the same time to reach the correct statement.

To assist in acquiring the skill to understand, use and manipulate the unspoken communication, I have included the following non-verbal situations. These are basic silent forms of conversation that are exposed in daily interactions. I have tried proving the unspoken word wrong since 1986 . . . it hasn't happened yet!

The following are a few sample situations of silent conversation you probably see every day:

Fig: 34

## Handshake #1

Handshake with hands side-by-side means equality. No one has the "upper hand." Also observe:

Position:  Are both their feet pointed toward you?

Posture:  Both persons are standing straight; not bent at waist

Gesture:  Positive handshake?

Distance:  Are you being kept at "arms" length?

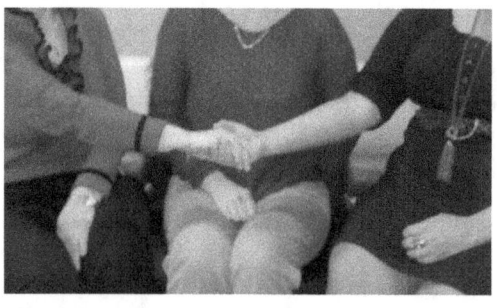

Fig:35

## Handshake #2

Hand over the top signifies control and aggression. Also observe:

Position:    Lady leaning in front of another lady

Posture:    One lady leaning in; the other lady leaning back

Gesture:    Both looking at each other's face

Distance:    18" to 4'; Personal Zone

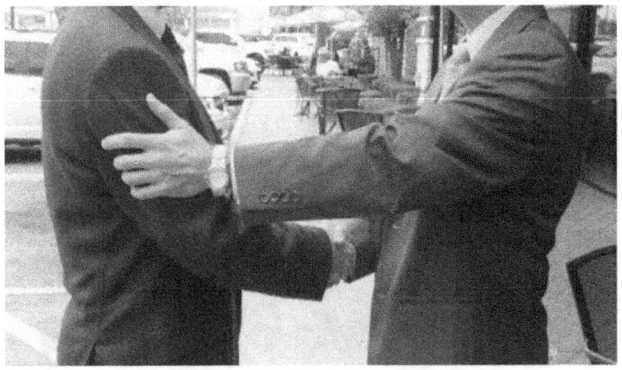

Fig: 36

## Handshake #3

Left hand on arm signifies emotion. The higher up the arm; the more emotion is demonstrated.

Position:    Both bodies are facing each other

Posture:    Equality handshake

Gesture:    Left hand for added expression

Distance:    18" to 4'; Personal Zone

Fig: 37

## "I think I want to talk"

This is the 1st of three positions shown when a person wants to talk.

Position:   Seated or standing

Posture:   Seated erect

Gesture:   Hands folded with fingers interlocked at waist level

Distance:   Any of the four zones

Fig:38

## "I know I want to talk"

This is the 2<sup>nd</sup> of three positions shown when a person
wants to talk.

Position:   Seated or standing
Posture:    Seated erect
Gesture:    Hands folded with fingers interlocked at
            shoulder height.  You should allow the per-
            son to talk or face consequences.
Distance:   Any of the four zones

Fig: 39

## "I want to talk now!"

This is the 3rd of three positions shown when a person wants to talk.

Position:   Seated or standing

Posture:   Seated erect

Gesture:   Hands folded with fingers interlocked in front of mouth. Now they are upset you didn't let them talk.

Distance:   Any of the four zones

Fig: 40

## "I don't believe they said that!"

Position:  Standing
Posture:  Standing erect
Gesture:  Finger to mouth; arm across chest holding arm; sideways glance.
Distance:  Any of the four zones

Fig: 41

## "I don't see it that way"

Position:    Standing

Posture:     Standing erect with head looking down

Gesture:     Finger to eye; eyes looking down and to the
             right; right side of the brain is the creative
             side

Distance:    Any of the four zones

Fig: 42

## "Did I hear that correctly"

Position:    Standing or sitting

Posture:    Standing erect; head tilted to the right creative side

Gesture:    Finger to ear; sideways glance.

Distance:    Any of the four zones

Fig: 43

## Manager speaking with team member

Seated directly across from a person normally means an aggressive and defensive position.

Position:  Sitting across from each other with desk between; manager's chair slightly higher

Posture:  Manager seated leaning in; subordinate seated erect

Gesture:  Hands palms down with glasses as a barrier; slight sideways glance

Distance:  4' to 12'; Social Zone

Fig: 44

## <u>Someone is happy with their decision!!</u>

Position:   Seated

Posture:   Leaning back increasing distance; jacket is unbuttoned

Gesture:   Smiling with teeth showing; hands to back of head

Distance:   Any of the four zones

Fig: 45

## Typical eye block: "are you still there?!"

Position: Standing next to the other person
Posture: Standing erect with head looking down
Gesture: Hand covering closed eyes; head looking away; no smile
Distance: Any of the four zones

Fig: 46

## "Do these women really want to talk to one another?"

Position:  Seated
Posture:   Seated with legs together
Gesture:   Legs are pointed away from the next person
Distance:  0" to 18"; Intimate Zone

The answer is, "No, neither lady wants to talk to the other because their legs are crossed away from the next person. Try crossing your legs toward and away from the person next to you. Notice how your body is forced to move in the direction of the leg cross. Let's look at another example of "pointing feet."

Fig: 47

## <u>What person wants to leave? Why?</u>

Position:   Standing
Posture:    Legs spread
Gesture:    One person's foot pointed at another person; another person's foot pointed away from group;
Distance:   Vary between 0" and 12'; Intimate and Personal Zones

Interesting how people talk without uttering a word!! The person understanding the unspoken word has a huge advantage. A few facts to close this section:

- The unspoken word does not know how to lie.
- The spoken word knows how to lie.
- Only interpret the unspoken word when the other person does not know their movements are being observed.

- Always use the person's "3-step movements" when deciphering the current non-verbal expressions.
- IMPORTANT: The "3-step movements" are the actions shown before, during and after that moment of observed silent conversation. An example would be a person listening to a discussion which will lead to a decision.

## *Before making the decision the situation is:*

| | |
|---|---|
| Position: | Seated directly across for the presenter and leaning in; interested in what is said |
| Posture: | Arms and legs are crossed; not open-minded |
| Gesture: | Tight-lipped smile and raised eyebrows; showing the attitudes of objection or skepticism |
| Distance: | Across a table which is 30"-40" from the person; Personal Zone |

## *While making the decision the situation is:*

| | |
|---|---|
| Position: | Seated directly across for the presenter and now, sitting straight; removing themselves from the discussion |
| Posture: | Arms and legs are crossed; not open-minded |
| Gesture: | Eyes looking up; pierced mouth; rubbing the chin; the person is in decision making mode |
| Distance: | Across a table which is 30"-40" from the person; Personal Zone |

## *After making the decision the situation is:*

Position: Seated directly across for the presenter, but now, leaning back; totally removed themselves from the discussion

Posture: Legs are crossed; arms clasped behind head; a display of personal ease or comfort

Gesture: Smile on their face; happy with their decision

Distance: The person is now leaning back in their chair increasing the space from the presenter to 60"; Social Zone

Their decision clearly is not one of agreement.

90% - P & M - 8:1 - 4:30 - 15:30 - 66% - 86%

STOP!!! Take five minutes and identify how this new information can improve your personal and professional communication performance.

Fig: 48

## CHAPTER TEN

......................................................................

## 86%

And now we come to the chapter that contains the conclusion of all the facts contained in this great manifesto!! Just what does 86:9 mean? The answer is the final fact, the undoubted reason, the scientifically proven reason why we have to change from audio to visual based communication. Don't keep talking to yourself!!

86:9 is a short cut for you to remember "86% of what a person remembers is seen and only 9% is heard!!"

The main goal of any communication is to have the audience remember what the presenter needs them to remember. As past research reveals, until recently it was believed the spoken word triggered the memory system. Past research involving Visual-Short and Long-Term Memory were rudimentary as compared with today's experiments. More importantly, measuring the actions of the brain was archaic at best.

Today it is acknowledged that 86% of what a person retains is visual; only 9% is auditory. What caused the major shift in the initial beliefs? With the introduction of higher computer speeds and capacities which began in the early 2000's, the MRI became the measuring tool for the memory process controlled by the various function of the brain.

A notable event occurred in 2003, when the Nobel Prize was won by Paul C. Lauterbur and Peter Mansfield for their discoveries of using MRIs as a diagnostic tool; which also aided in the scientific credibility of the measurement of brain functions and the memory system. The purpose of their research was to determine whether auditory or visual short-term memory is held for a longer and more accurate duration. An analysis of variance indicated the visual presentation was recalled more accurately than the auditory presentation.

Some other scientific proven factors supporting The 86% Visual Advantage are:

- The visual impulses were seen and heard through rehearsal maintenance in the brain. However, the auditory process was only heard, making that a more difficult process to perform.
- There is a variation among the visual and auditory words. Since the words have a main effect, people find it easier to recall the visual words with more accuracy. The same can be said about the length of words.
- Short-Term Memory has been thought to be an auditory process. After doing this study, it seems as though Short-Term Memory can be thought of as a visual process as well. This becomes apparent because the visual experiment recalled more words

correctly. In fact, the visual test did relatively better than the auditory experiment.

Without getting further into the depth of a scientific discussion, let's look at a very simple example. Let's assume the brain remembers 100 new bits of information. Applying the proven ratio between visual and verbal retention let us look at the results. 86 bits of that new information is remembered through vision, and only 9 new items were retained from hearing.

Talk about talking to yourself!!!

90% - P & M - 8:1 - 4:30 - 15:30 - 66% - 86%

STOP!!! Take five minutes and identify how this new information can improve your personal and professional communication performance.

Fig: 49

.........................................................................

## CHAPTER ELEVEN

# HOW TO USE THE 86% VISUAL SOLUTION: MINIMIZE THE UNFINISHED WORK WEEK

This entire discussion has centered around the fact visual communication is far more effective than hearing the spoken word. Using this fact in communicating will reduce The Unfinished Work Week and allow personal time to be regained. Logically it is realized this conclusion calls for change. That is a word most people do not like not to hear. I remind you of a more tragic word . . . complacency. That is the false comfort feeling negating the need for further education. Complacency allows competition to succeed at your expense.

Remember the quote from Confucius, "only the most wise and most stupid of people never change." Which are you?

To begin the change from verbal to visual emphasized communication, seven sets of numbers must be memorize and understood. These digits will be the litmus test for the Key Topic to be retained by the audience.

90% - P & M - 8:1 - 4:30 - 15:30 - 86% - 66%

Understanding these numbers is critical to committing to alter the current communication process. The next step is to remind you of the meaning of these numbers.

1. The goal: to be remembered (90% of information is forgotten in 8 hours).
2. Identify the Key Topics (personal and meaningful: significant information which positively affects an individual's motives as they pertain to performance).
3. Allow a minimum of 8-10 minutes to discuss (Short- Term Working Memory) each Key Topic (8:1: brain has the capacity to remember 8 new pieces of information in 1 hour).
4. Keep the supporting messages simple: Remember the processing of information (4:30: the mind can process 4 verbal items in 30 seconds; 15:30: the mind can process 15 visual items in 30 seconds).
5. Display honest silent conversation and "read" the audience to maintain credibility (66% of all face-to-face communication is non-verbal).
6. Use the same visuals (more than once) that support the Key Topic (86% of what a person remembers is visual).

# Visual Text Messages

The next step is to examine how the 86% Visual Solution actually works in business situations. It was interesting to uncover the fact that over 50% of an average work day is devoted to managing Email. Is this a form of visual communication? Most certainly it is. Text messaging should be included in this category as well. Most text messages are short and concise without containing many Key Topics. In other words, most text messages have a short memory life. Maybe it contains a time to meet? Confirm an appointment? Text messaging is not yet an accepted formal form of business communication. But think of how good the communication process is. One subject is addressed in less than 30 seconds. If this is a Key Topic, the next step is to discuss the topic. In this case, follow-up text messages during the day that support The Key Message can be the process to have the audience remember what you want them to remember.

## *Example of Text Messaging*

You: "Just read the 86% Visual Advantage."

Them: "What was it about?"

You: "86% of what you remember is seen."

Them: "Never heard that before."

Later in the day:

You: "Did you know the brain has the capacity to remember only 8 new items in an hour!"

Them: "Where did you get that from?"

You: "The 86% Visual Advantage."

Of course there would be a substitute Key Topic. The discussion can be maintained for as long as both participants are taking part in the conversation. A new Key Topic could be reminding an associate of information owed to you. First, state the Key Topic. Then, follow-up by sending reasons why it is important for the information to be received. A reminder; what may be personal and meaningful to you, may not be personal and meaningful to your associate. It is up to you to make it a "significant motive to perform." Remember, one Key Topic per text.

Just by the nature of this type of communication, a text message can be easily included in the visual working memory until the Key Topic event has taken place. Then the information will become part of the 90% forgotten group.

Before going further, get a good understanding of what a Key Topic is; something easy to remember. Yes, the complete definition is, "significant information which positively affects an individual's motives as they pertain to performance." But that is a lot of words to remember. Focus only on the *key words*, just like a Google search does. In this case the *key words* are "*significant motive to perform*." Those words give meaning to the definition.

Here is another example of "significant motive to perform."

Suppose the director of the department has asked a fellow manager to work with your group on an assignment. A deadline has been imposed to have the project completed by Friday. This manager has a reputation for procrastination. Realizing if the time schedule is not kept, extra pressure is put on your department which may affect some other deadlines. What do you do? Be reactive and sit back and let the manager come to you at the last minute? Or be proactive and protect the team from unneeded stress?

You: "Hey Ben, what information do you need from us?"

Ben: "Don't worry about it. Plenty of time."

Next day.

You: "Just another reminder on that mutual assignment."

Ben: "I'll get back to you."

Next day.

You: "Just was handed additional work for my team."

Ben: "The information I need won't take a lot of time."

You: "Ben, I am telling you, the new assignment takes priority over yours. If you miss the deadline, you may end up having to get the data yourself."

Ben: "I don't know how to get it."

You: "Then when can we get together?"

Ben: "Today."

Congratulations!! The goal was accomplished. Use visual text messaging to make the audience remember what you want them to remember. Both controlled and stimuli types of attention were used to have the Key Topic enter the Visual- Working Memory checkpoint. It was remembered for as long as it is needed it to be remembered exercising the 15:30 processing rule. Since graphic smiley faces or frowns cannot be used in a business setting, choose your words wisely so the message is not misinterpreted.

90% - P & M - 8:1 - 4:30 - 15:30 - 86% - 66%

STOP!!! Take five minutes and identify how this new information can improve your personal and professional communication performance.

## Visual Email

Visual Email is the long version of texting and is also an excepted business form of communication. When are Emails used? Here is the beginning of a long list:

1. Invitation to a meeting
2. Agendas of meetings
3. Summary of meetings
4. Summary of phone calls
5. Summary of webinars
6. Request for needed information
7. Forward needed information

Email has replaced a large portion of phone conversations. Isn't that something? Technology, unknowingly, is helping in the switch from verbal to visual communication. And you thought this was going to be a hard transition. The computer has changed the method of conversation. This means you must learn how to use this method effectively or lose to competition. Think of associates not understanding the value of basic applications of smart phones. Have they advanced in this ever-changing corporate world?

A reminder, over 50% of an employee's time is spent managing Emails. . . . an average of approximately 115 daily! *That's the average, which means some people have over 200 Emails a day to read and reply.* Why is the percentage so high? Think of your own situation. How many Emails are received that are a recap of past Emails? How many Emails are unnecessary? How many Emails are not answered? How many Emails are ignored?

Understanding the majority of time is spent in non-face-to-face communication, means the brain must interpret what these visual, type-written words really mean. It is imperative to help the other person open the Email and retain the included Key Topic by following the Memory Rules.

This is where the Key Topic . . personal and meaningful . . . significant – motive – perform . . . becomes even more important. Think of how the brain prioritizes all these 115 messages; by importance to you. Does an Email from your supervisor automatically receive top priority or does a message containing needed information for your team to complete a task affecting other employees take the top spot?

We all know the answer, "the supervisor can wait!"

The Key Topic must be the subject line. Then the body of the message can be addressed. Warning: the brain does not like to see a lot of words strung together. It is too much work deciphering what is and what is not important (4:30; 15:30). The memory system can be overloaded very quickly which only leads to the Key Topic not being retained. Why? Because the path followed has gone down the "slippery slope" greased with unneeded words. Attention span "slipped" from control, to stimuli and finally hits bottom at arousal. All that time spent writing an Email that doesn't even get read or remembered. What a waste.

Start by reviewing some key facts to come to a logical conclusion.

- An average person can read 250 words per minute. (31)
- An average Email contains 100 words.(32)
- The brain can only process 7 written words in 30 seconds (this allows for the time the brain does not have to spell the "heard" word).

- The brain can remember one new bit of information in one to eight minutes.

Question: How many words are needed for the brain to remember one new bit of information? And it better not be 250!

If an average Email contains 100 words, it can be read in 25 seconds. But are all these words needed to have the Key Topic comprehended? No, because the average sentence contains sixteen to twenty-five words.(33) This is how an effective Email can be created in 100 words or less. The subject line immediately is supported with information that *significantly* affects the *motive* to *perform*. Even if one sentence is devoted to each supporting topic, the shortest length of the Email would be 48 words. This is much less than the current 100 words per Email.

It is known the comprehension rate is 25% of what is heard.(34) If this is true, we need 28 words for the brain to process 7 items in 30 seconds or 56 words per minute. That is getting pretty close to that 48 word Email. With the big exception: the 56 words should be read in 1 minute, not in 20 seconds! Limit the words per Email to 48-56 in order to have the recipient remember one Key Topic.

Knowing the brain can only processes 7 new items of information in 30 seconds, reading a one hundred word Email in 25 seconds can create information overload. Once the brain has attained capacity it "takes a rest" and those favorite M&M's begin to fall out of the bowl!

If the message is to be remembered, keep the Email brief and use words selectively to support the subject line Key Topic. You have the responsibility to keep the brain happy and not overloaded with unneeded words.

Before composing the Email identify what should be said as briefly as possible. Remember, this is not an English class. No one is grading this term paper. This is all about effective communication using the Memory Rules. Use some of the following:

a. Phrases replace sentences
b. Use short words (average 5 letters) when possible
c. Brief supporting bullet points
d. Long messages are scanned
e. Short messages are read
f. Realize the recipient can't see or hear the tone of the correspondence

Our goal is to be more effective and productive in the primary source of corporate communication. You want to take back personal time by reducing The Unfinished Work Week. Here is a sample of how this can be done.

The following is a random Email originating in a large corporation. The assignment is to make this an efficient correspondence. The goal is to be included in the 10% that is remembered during the day.

### Example:

"Regarding Spain, we get virtually no direct employee contacts. And, I would suggest that there is not a typical level of routine HR outreach to us. Employees are encouraged to go to local HR. And, as you know, employee self service is not typically a suggested, or even an available option in many cases.

Although the types of employee inquiries would be the same across all locations, I doubt looking at one location would be representative of typical volumes across Spain. If the effort will be to simply track HR inquiry volume (with little or no detailed reporting), despite the local burden, we should consider a broader sample than just one site.

However, if I had to pick one, as one would expect, we should look at Derby.

Regardless whether we're looking at Spain or the US, perhaps in lieu of selective local tracking, and the associated local burdens, could we craft a quick survey monkey questionnaire to the HR field organization. At most a couple of questions- which could be answered without any formal research. For example...(1) In a typical week (other than during open enrollment) approximately how many benefit program related inquiries do you receive from employees? Consider all types of plans and forms of contact (i.e., calls, emails, in person)..

(2) Considering all types of inquiries, and the various levels of assistance you provide, approximately how many of these are you able to fully handle locally without further support from other parties ( i.e., Salem Benefits, Salem Payroll, insurance companies, etc,)?

One last thought....Do we know for certain that some level of this tracking is not already being done? I've seen in my past experience some HR organizations that track certain local metrics to measure quantity and qualtity of "customer" service. Number of contacts with HR related to benefits is one of the tracked items."

That was only 309 words! Which means the Email can be read in 90 seconds. But how much could be remembered? What were the Key Topics?

I believe the last paragraph should have been the entire Email.

Why waste time to add input if it is not needed?

## *Example:*

"Is HR tracking being completed? Some companies include benefits as a tracked item." That is a grand total of 13 words.

Let's assume the answer is no. This means the Email has to be perused and the Key Topics identified. What should the recipient remember about this Email? The Key Topic must be personal and meaningful. You know, *significant* information positively affecting the *motive* to *perform*. Here is my list:

1. Goal: Determine Spain's HR volume call effecting different locations
2. Use Derby but a broader survey should be taken.
3. To gather more accurate data a "Survey Monkey " could be sent to the HR field organizations

Incorporating the brain-controlled Memory Rules, the revised Email could be written in the following manner:

## *Example:*

"Bob:
These are the requested suggestions:

1. Goal: Determine Spain's HR volume call effecting different locations
2. Use Derby but a broader survey should be taken.

3.  To gather more accurate data a "Survey Monkey" could be sent to the HR field organizations Get back to me with any questions. Alice Murphy"

See, it can be done.  A 309 word Email was reduced to 52 words without losing any meaning of the message.

Instead of eliminating Email as Atos has done, or declare "Email free Fridays" like Intel, maybe employees should learn how to use this communication tool correctly. The easiest learning technique would require the company's IT Department to limit the number of words in an Email.

Just think if everyone learned efficient, memorable Email messaging how much of The Unfinshed Work Week could be eliminated. This results in more personal time.

90% - P & M - 8:1 - 4:30 - 15:30 - 86% - 66%

STOP!!! Take five minutes and identify how this new information can improve your personal and professional communication performance.

## Webinars

What has been taking the place of conference calls?  The answer is webinars.  This is the visual vs. verbal confrontation in the virtual world.  The telephone offers only the hearing of words; while the webinar combines audio with written information in the form of slides or PowerPoint presentations. It can be a very effect means of communication.  Effective only if the webinar is created under the brain-controlled Memory Rules. Otherwise, whenever this type of meeting is held The Unfinished Work Week becomes more of a reality.

Think of webinars as virtual PowerPoint presentations with a major exception: the presenter cannot see the entire audience. I call this a major exception because the presenter cannot "read" the attention and interest level of the attendees in order to adjust the presentation to be remembered. It is well known in both conference calls and webinars, the attendees activate the mute button. Why? So no one can hear them completing other assignments, even speaking with people, while supposedly "attending" the conference. The "unmute" button is only pushed when the topic being discussed pertains to their department. Talk about a waste of time!! Question: why include employees in meetings in which subject matter is discussed that doesn't concern them? Once again, it only adds to The Unfinished Work Week.

As far as creating and presenting a memorable webinar, follow the suggestions listed under the PowerPoint Presentations later in this chapter. Webinars are still a strong way to have your Key Topic retained. Why? Because everything is visual. Which means The 86% Visual Solution is working.

90% - P & M - 8:1 - 4:30 - 15:30 - 86% - 66%

STOP!!! Take five minutes and identify how this new information can improve your personal and professional communication performance.

## Meetings: In-Person and Video Conferencing

All the In-Person and Virtual Visual Meetings are grouped together. Technology has been a forerunner of switching verbal to visual conversation by replacing phone calls with the visual written word in texts and Emails. Now technology has added to expensive video conferencing with no or low cost video programs like SKYPE and ooVoo. These visual programs are even available on smart phones!! Do these corporate giants add these programs at a whim, or is much market research completed before including this software? The simple truth is people are more comfortable seeing the person they are speaking with. . . . especially supervisors. Why?

As was discussed in Chapter Nine, 66% of conversation is non-verbal. Combine this information with the fact 86% of what a person remembers is seen and it is easy to understand why the brain likes this very personal type of communication. The body speaks volumes about how a message is being given and received. Unlike verbal interaction, the unspoken word doesn't lie. Both the presenter and audience can immediately see the attention levels of each other as Key Topics are discussed. This allows for instant adjustments to be made if the goal of having the audience remember what the presenter wants remembered is to be attained.

The power of visual communication is extraordinary. Think of how unknowingly it is used every day. Every second of the day! You talk about interpreting what a person says every day.

"Oh, did you see the look in their eyes!!"

"I could just tell, Tina didn't agree with Bill."

"It seems like Alan was just going through the motions."

I cannot impress upon you more emphatically the need to have a working knowledge of silent communication. Agreement to road blocks can be controlled before they become a big issue. Best of all, the comfortable atmosphere can be controlled that is needed if the audience is to trust in the Key Topic.

Remember, this type of communication can happen at any moment. Whether sitting in an office or travelling in a car, the silent language will be seen and heard loud and clear!!

In-Person and Virtual Visual Meeting Rules:

- Use written and pictorial tools during the meeting
- Always send a short follow-up Email just listing the Key Topics discussed as soon as the meeting concludes.

Virtual Visual Meetings are just like in-person meetings with the exception you are not actually there.

90% - P & M - 8:1 - 4:30 - 15:30 - 66% - 86%

STOP!!! Take five minutes and identify how this new information can improve your personal and professional communication performance.

## PowerPoint Presentations

This is the most powerful way to effectively communicate by using the:

a. Heard word (4:30)
b. Visual written word (7:30)
c. Visual graphics (15:30)
d. Visual audience silent conversation (66%)
e. Visual presenter's non-verbal communication (66%)

The brain is so happy not to work as hard to interpret what is being communicated. All the ingredients for the memory process to perform easily, accurately and to full capacity are present (8:1). What could go wrong!?!

Fig:50

A thing called "Death by PowerPoint." That is what could go wrong.

Employees are upset with the waste of time involved in sitting through mandatory "poor" PowerPoint presentations. What constitutes a poor PowerPoint Performance? The audience complains about:(32)

a. No clear purpose of the presentation
b. No flow of ideas
c. Too many fonts used
d. Text so small no one could read it
e. Full sentences instead of bullet points

f. Slides hard to see because of color choice
g. Moving/flying text or graphics
h. Annoying use of sounds
i. Overly complex charts or diagrams
j. Graphic images do not match the slide topic

This list will continue to grow as long as these presentations are not created under the Memory Rules. But before presenting how to use this ideal form of communication correctly, let's find out how costly Death by PowerPoint can be.

Noted author and authority of PowerPoint presentations, Dave Paradi, calculates the cost of poor presentations to be no less than $45,000 per presentation for a company with at least 250 employees. If the company has two presentations a day the loss becomes $90,000. And if ten presentations are given, the contribution to the unproductive work week is only $450,000.(35) How many weekends do employees have to work to make up that amount of negative productivity!?!

Think about this situation. A big asset has been made a big liability. The best communication tool is limited due to the lack of understanding how to use it.

But something can be done to improve the lethal situation.

Once again The 86% Visual Solution must be used in creating the presentation. First, eliminate all those reasons constituting a "poor" PowerPoint presentation. The following are rather simple to resolve:

a. Just use one or two different fonts
b. To ensure everyone can read the text, don't go below 28 font size.

c. Slides hard to see because of color choice. The font colors should be in major contrast to the background color. By the way, yellow is the "remember" color.

d. Never use moving/flying text or graphics which may draw more attention than the topic on the slide.

e. Try to avoid the use of sounds.

f. The brain doesn't like overly complex charts or diagrams. In other words, you have created information overload and the brain goes to arousal attention.

After completing the easy fix, apply the Memory Rules and types of attention needed to have the Key Message remembered. That is the goal of any communication.

## Step 1

Establish the amount of time that will be devoted for the presentation. Then apply the 8:1 rule. If one hour has been set aside, then present only 8 new bits of information. If you have 2 hours, then plan no more than 16 Key Topics. On the reverse, a 30 minute presentation means no more than 4 new items can be introduced.

## Step 2

Prioritize the Key Topics the audience has to remember. This is not easy as it sounds. The Key Topics must be personal and meaningful to the audience. The attendees decide the *significant* information that positively affects their *motive* to *perform*. Also, the Key Topics must complement each other and be presented in a logical order or flow. Hint: the wise person does not play to capacity all the time. In other words, instead of using 8:1 Key Topic ratio, implement something less like 6:1 to ensure the Key Topics presented are remembered.

## Step 3

How many slides? The answer is a direct result of the average number of minutes for the brain to process the Key Topic from short term memory to working and/or long term memory. If the conservative average ratio of 6:1 is used, allow 10 minutes to present one Key Topic. Slides contain information to support and explain the *significant* information, personal *motive* and result of *performance* associated with the Key Topic. At the *most* reserve 2 slides per Key Topic. That means no more than 16 slides for a 1 hour presentation. This also dictates 10 minutes of conversation per Key Topic. Enough time for the brain to remember what you want remembered.

## Step 4

How much information on a slide? Remember, the goal of the slide is to enhance the retention of the Key Topic. So, no more than 5 bullet points in phrase, not sentence, format. This allows for the use of graphics that support the message of the slide and still meet the minimum 28 font size. Be careful with those graphics and pictures. Do not make them the "attention getter" of the slide. They are in a support position, so the memory can see the picture instead of visualizing the words.

**Strategic Preliminary Information Employee**

- What are your personal goals?
- What are your career goals?
- How are these goals achieved?
- How do you effect goal attainment of other employees?
- Who is your most important customer?
- Who is helping this customer succeed?
- Why do you work for the company?

Fig: 51

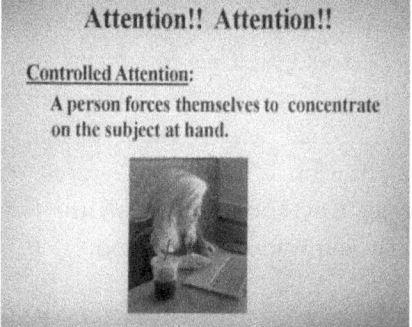

**Attention!! Attention!!**

Controlled Attention:

A person forces themselves to concentrate on the subject at hand.

Fig: 52

# Step 5

How does the slide come to life? One slide can turn into multiple slides just by inserting bullet points one at a time, instead of listing them all at once. In fact, this is a rule that has to be followed. Remember who is in control!!! It's not the presenter. It is the brain receptors of your audience.

The Memory Rules state the brain does not like to see or hear a lot of words at one time. I remind you, 4:30, 7:30

and 15:30 are not times of the day. They are the memory ratios. The easier the brain can process information, the more efficient and effective the memory process becomes.

Remember this phrase: "Key Topic: See, Discuss, Remember."

Use this philosophy when introducing each bulleted phrase. This allows for the proper digesting of the information to be retained. To review:

<u>Key Topic</u>: Personal and meaningful: *significant* information positively affecting the *motive* to *perform*.

    a.  <u>See</u> the Key Topic on the slide.

    b.  **<u>Discuss </u>**the seen Key Topic. Set aside 8-10 minutes to use bulleted information to help the audience retain the message. The word is discuss, not lecture.

    c.  **<u>Remember </u>**the seen and discussed Key Topic. In order to insure the information is retained engage the audience to receive their input. By having the audience summarize the Key Topic in their own words, you know the message was at least retained in working short term memory.

# Step 6

Help the audience retain all the discussed key topics. As each Key Topic is introduced, insert the title on each following slide. By the end of an hour presentation, the last slide should be the summary page of each Key Topic. Use the rules discussed in Step 5 to ensure the 6-8 main titles have been retained. An example of this memory strategy has been used throughout this document. Haven't you noticed the cryptic message at the end of each chapter?

Did you notice where the message is placed in regard to the last paragraph, which also appears at the end of each chapter. The message is there for a very important reason: Key Topic: See. Discuss. Remember.

## Step 7

Now that the presentation has been created under the Memory Rules and rehearsed, it is time to give the performance. It is time to look back to Chapter 9 and the discussion under Virtual Visual Meetings. Now is the opportunity to use the visual tools of the written word, supporting graphics and the body to have the message remembered. If the Key Topic is not remembered . . . it is your fault.

### *Obstacles effecting In-Person Meetings, Video Conferencing and PowerPoint Presentations*

Now is the time to be conscious of two important barriers to success: a) types of attention; and, b) Roadblocks to Agreement. The different types of attention were discussed way back in Chapter Two. So a quick reminder, at any meeting you want to see a combination of controlled and stimuli attention.

Fig: 53 Fig: 54

Controlled - Concentration    Stimuli – external influence

It was noted the adult concentration span is 20 minutes. But that doesn't mean 20 minutes of controlled attention. Think of how you react in meetings even if the main topic is personal and meaningful. Guaranteed at first controlled attention mode is in effect. Then within those 20 minutes the mind drifts to other things you have to accomplish during the day. Then, if the presenter is really good, they notice the need to either change the subject or give a mental break.

No matter what type of meeting it is: webinar, Virtual Visual Meeting, in-person or PowerPoint presentations, allow the audience time to "stay in touch" with their daily activities. Let them know there will be 10 minute mental breaks every fifty minutes. This fact reassures the audience to devote controlled attention to the meeting. If mental breaks are not allowed, I guarantee the audience will fall into the abyss, called arousal attention.

Fig: 55

Good luck getting this meeting to be productive!! It should never have gotten to this point.

Roadblocks to an agreement are three basic attitudes every person displays when some type of disagreement is believed to be present. These attitudes are:

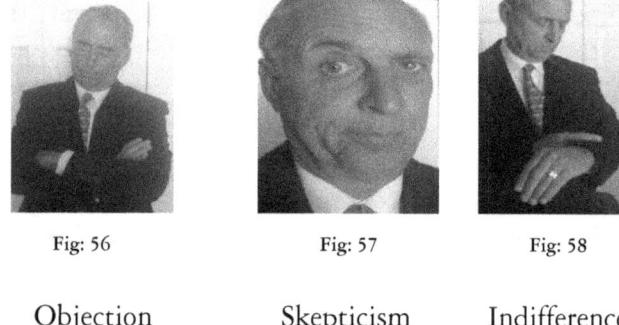

| Fig: 56 | Fig: 57 | Fig: 58 |

| Objection | Skepticism | Indifference |

Each attitude is visually apparent before verbally stated. Once the person speaks, the attitude has become a rather large Roadblock to Agreement.

It is your responsibility to notice:

a. Objection: Is simply an opposition to a statement. This attitude is normally formed due to a misunderstanding of the information being presented. Watch out, this may become confrontational.

b. Skepticism: Questions or doubts the stated subject material. In other words, they don't believe you!!

c. Indifference: A lack of interest because of no perceived value of the information presented. They can't wait to leave!!

As was mentioned, A&A, Attentions and Attitudes exist during every communication. The drawback to non-visual communication is the uncomfortable atmosphere is not seen developing. The mole hill becomes a mountain blocking the memory of the Key Topic. This only adds to The Unfinished Work Week.

On the other hand, all types of visual communication allow you to control the attention spans and attitudes. Begin with acknowledging the attitude exists and then remove the attitude before it becomes the Key Topic of the meeting.

This concludes the directions on how to implement the visual tools which result in 86% of what a person remembers is seen. It is the most important chapter of this masterpiece as it addresses the visual tools of:

a. Visual worded text messaging

b. Visual worded Email messaging

c. Webinars

    **d.**  In-person and Virtual Visual Meetings
    **e.**  PowerPoint Presentations

Use these visual technology enhanced tools correctly and the 30% Wasted Work Week can become obsolete.

90% - P & M - 8:1 - 4:30 - 15:30 - 66% - 86%

STOP!!! Take five minutes and identify how this new information can improve your personal and professional communication performance.

Fig: 59

........................................................

## CHAPTER TWELVE

# A FEW RANDOM THOUGHTS

Originally my research was how the memory process affected sales and negotiations. Questioning why the visual-verbal ratio was so high. I mean 86% of what a person remembers is seen as opposed to 9% being heard. This is huge!!

What is the business benefit of The 86% Visual Solution? I couldn't see the forest through the trees!! Then, voila, it happened. What is the main reason for The Unfinished Work Week? Answer: ineffective communication.

Why are most of us poor communicators? I will not use the word reasons, BUT will use the word EXCUSES. It can always be said:

- They didn't teach me visual communication in school
- Visual communication was not offered in college
- The correct way to write a memorable text or Email was not included in the Microsoft installation CD

- The correct way to use PowerPoint also was not included in the installation CD
- Even the "Apple makes it easy" Steve Jobs didn't address the subject of effective communication using today's technology

The simple truth is technical interaction tools are not used effectively and efficiently. If we could reduce the time managing Emails and the number "poor" PowerPoint presentations, think of how much more personal time could be enjoyed instead of used to make up for non-productivity!!

As stated earlier, commitment to moving out of your "comfort zone" is a must. I just completed presenting full day sessions on sales negotiations, and was asked, "of all the Key Topics discussed, which was most important?" The answer, "acknowledge and commit to change." If not, you are at the mercy of complacency. Why be left behind?

William I. Weiss former CEO of Ameritech stated this realistic phrase concerning change, "create an internal explosion that begins to get people's attention, drawn to the fact that the future is going to be different." Of course, Mr. Weiss is correct. The fact is the future is going to be different. Knowing this, it is mandatory to be different to succeed in the future.

But there will always be one constant fact. In order to alter the usual manner of conducting business in the future, everything new item must be processed by the brain-controlled memory. That will never change. Since that is the topic of this book, the 86% Visual Solution will always exist.

Thank you for taking the time to read, review and discuss the information offered in this visual written presentation.

Please visit our websites at www.86percentvisualadvantage. com and www.theunfinishedworkweek.com.

90% - P & M - 8:1 - 4:30 - 15:30 - 66% - 86%

STOP!!! Take five minutes and identify how this new information can improve your personal and professional communication performance.

**CHAPTER THIRTEEN**

....................................................................

# ABOUT THE AUTHOR

Andrew Gateriewictz has been a guest lecturer at The Wharton School of the University of Pennsylvania because of his the unique ability to use the visual communication process to increase the productivity of employees in the corporate world.

What makes him an authority? Mr. Gateriewictz held positions of sales representative, branch manager, regional manager and vice president of sales and marketing for companies in the Fortune 500. This experience formed the business acumen which has resulted in a successful consulting career.

In 1986 he began research study in the field of neuro-linguistics. On September 19, 1993, The Philadelphia Inquirer recognized his work as an authority in understanding and the use of body language throughout the selling process. His work in this field is protected by U.S. Copyrights.

In 1993 Mr. Gateriewictz created a consulting company, Strategees and Associates, Inc., which included sales, marketing and visual communication programs. These programs have been used by employees of companies such as Andersen Windows, The Home Depot, PNC Bank, Bank Five, IBM, Lucent Technologies, Radio Disney and Avaya Telecommunications.

In addition to speaking at The Wharton School, he also is an adjunct professor for Gloucester Community College (NJ), Hillsborough Community College (FL) and Jacksonville Community College (AL).

Becoming aware of the exorbitant amount of time employees spend trying to keep up with their corporate responsibilities, Mr. Gateriewictz decided to create The Unfinished Work Week: Lost Personal Time to improve efficiency and productivity in the work place. This allows more personal time for families instead of devoting week nights and weekends to catching up on uncompleted assignments.

The common causes for unproductive time are: a) unclear objectives; b) lack of team communication; c) ineffective meetings, and d) unclear priorities. These reasons fall under one common denominator – ineffective visual interaction. That is what this book is about: how improved visual interaction can improve The Unfinished Work Week.

This book is for people *committed* to improving their professional communication results. From sales people to CEOs and all positions in between, this manuscript contains beneficial information.

The information forming the basis for this book is protected by U.S. Copyright Numbers TX 7-244-061 and TX7-220-520 assigned to Andrew Gateriewictz.

# FOOTNOTES:

1. Tech Firm Implements Employee "Zero eMail" Policy
   http://abcnews.go.com/blogs/business/2011/11/tech-company-implements-employee-zero-email-policy/
2. The Microsoft Office Personal Productivity Challenge (PPC) March 2005
3. The Radicati Group, Inc. 2010 Email Statistics Report
4. INC. com, March 2, 2011
5. Dave Paradi, MBA, author of "The Visual Slide Revolution" and "102 Tips to Communicate More Effectively Using PowerPoint"
6. Dave Paradi, MBA, author of "The Visual Slide Revolution" and "102 Tips to Communicate More Effectively Using PowerPoint"
7. Baddely, Alan. "Memory," Science and Technology, vol. 10, pg. 674-675
   Baddely, Alan. Your Memory: A Users Guide, United Kingdom: Prion, 1993
8. Pease, Alan July 1, 1984, author of Signals

9. wiki.answers.com/Q/What is the Average number of words spoken

10. Neuroreport: 11 June 2003 - Volume 14 - Issue 8 - pp 1129-1133; Cognitive Neuroscience and Neuropsychology

11. Klingberg, Torkel, Oxford University Press 2009; "The Overflowing Brain"

12. Jenkins and Dallenback's Learning Curve, http://frank.itlab.us/forgetting/mtsu_forgetting/

13. Personal and Meaningful;www.human-memory.net/processes_encoding.html

14. Cowan, N. (2001). The magical number 4 in short-term memory: A reconsideration of mental storage capacity. Behavioral and Brain Sciences, 24(1).

15. Visual Short Term Working Memory, Intermediate visual store, http://en.wikipedia.org/wiki/Visual_short-term_memory

16. Pease, Alan July 1, 1984, author of Signals

17. Jenkins and Dallenback's Learning Curve, http://frank.itlab.us/forgetting/mtsu_forgetting

18. Franklin P. Jones Quotes - BrainyQuote www.brainyquote.com/quotes/authors/f/franklin_p_jones.

19. html Klingberg, Torkel, Oxford University Press 2009; "The Overflowing Brain"

20. Zefran Cochran, When Jack Welch was Deputy Director of Intelligence; https://www.cia.gov/library/center-for-the-study-of-intelligence/csi-publications/csi-studies/studies/vol48no3/article04.html

21. Arousal-Biased Competition in Perception and Memory

Mara Mather and Matthew R. Sutherland, Department of Psychology, University of Southern California, Los Angeles, CA www.usc.edu/projects/matherlab/pdfs/MatherSutherlandin press.pdf

22. http://en.wikipedia.org/wiki/Memory

23. Prahlad Gupta Word Learning and Verbal Short-Term Memory: A Computational Account; Beckman Institute for Advanced Science and Technology University of Illinois at Urbana-Champaign;Urbana, IL http://www.psychology.uiowa.edu/faculty/gupta/pdf/gupta.cogsci96.pdf

24. The Capacity of visual Short Term Memory; www.urop.uci.edu/SURP/.../SURP%20Social%20Sciences%204.pdfSimilarSligte IG, Scholte HS, Lamme VA.; V4 activity predicts the strength of visual short-term memory representations; Cognitive Neuroscience Group, Department of Psychology, University of Amsterdam, 1018WB Amsterdam, The Netherlands. I.G.Sligte@uva.nl http://www.ncbi.nlm.nih.gov/pubmed/19515911

25. Klingberg, Torkel, Oxford University Press 2009; "The Overflowing Brain"

26. Klingberg, Torkel, Oxford University Press 2009; "The Overflowing Brain"

27. http://en.wikipedia.org/wiki/Memory

28. Robert McCloskey Quotes; Thinkexist.com

29. Pease, Alan July 1, 1984, author of Signals

30. Words Per Minute FAQS http://www.turboread.com/wP.M._faqs.htm

31. Zoom International; Mind your language! Monitor, evaluate, improve!; www.zoomint.com

32. http://bluecentauri.com/tools/writer/sample.php

33. CM150 Listening: Our Most Used Communications Skill; extension.missouri.edu/Communications
34. The Microsoft Office Personal Productivity Challenge (PPC) March 2005
35. Dave Paradi, MBA, author of "The Visual Slide Revolution" and "102 Tips to Communicate More Effectively Using PowerPoint"

# REFERENCES:

- R. Lakoff, Language and Woman's Place (Harper, New York, 1975).
- L. Litosseliti, Gender and Language: Theory and Practice (Arnold, London, 2006).
- Brizendine, The Female Brain (Morgan Road, New York, 2006).
- M. Liberman, *Sex-Linked Lexical Budgets*, http://itre.cis.upenn.edu/~myl/languagelog/archives/003420.html (first accessed 12 December 2006).
- D. James, J. Drakich, in Gender and Conversational Interaction, D. Tannen, Ed. (Oxford Univ. Press, New York, 1993), pp. 281–313.
- P. Rayson, G. Leech, M. Hodges, Int. J. Corpus Linguist. 2, 133 (1997).
- M. R. Mehl, J. W. Pennebaker, M. Crow, J. Dabbs, J. Price, Behav. Res. Methods Instrum. Comput. 33, 517 (2001).
- Details on methods and analysis are available on *Science* Online.
- This research was supported by a grant from the National Institute of Mental Health (MH 52391).

We thank V. Dominguez, J. Greenberg, S. Holleran, C. Mehl, M. Peterson, and T. Schmader for their valuable feedback.

- Bennett, P. J., & Cortese, F. (1996). Masking of spatial frequency in visual memory depends on distal, not retinal, frequency. Vision Research, 36(2), 233-238.
- Blakemore, C., & Campbell, F. W. (1969). On the existence of neurons in the human visual system selectively sensitive to the orientation and size of retinal images. Journal of Physiology, 203, 237-260.
- Breitmeyer, B. (1984). Visual masking: An integrative approach. Oxford: Oxford University Press.
- Cermak, G. W. (1971). Short-term recognition memory for complex free-form figures. Psychonomic Science, 25(4), 209-211.
- Chua, F. K. (1990). The processing of spatial frequency and orientation information. Perception & Psychophysics, 47(1), 79-86.
- Cowan, N. (2001). The magical number 4 in short-term memory: A reconsideration of mental storage capacity. Behavioral and Brain Sciences, 24(1).
- DeValois, R. L., & DeValois, K. K. (1990). Spatial vision. Oxford: Oxford University Press.
- Greenlee, M. W., & Thomas, J. P. (1993). Simultaneous discrimination of the spatial frequency and contrast of periodic stimuli. Journal of the Optical Society of America A, 10(3), 395-404.
- Lee, B., & Harris, J. (1996). Contrast transfer characteristics of visual short-term memory. Vision Research, 36(14), 2159-2166.

- Luck, S. J., & Vogel, E. K. (1997). The capacity of visual working memory for features and conjunctions. Nature, 390, 279-281.
- Magnussen, S. (2000). Low-level memory processes in vision. Trends in Neurosciences, 23(6), 247-251.
- Magnussen, S., & Greenlee, M. W. (1992). Retention and disruption of motion information in visual short-term memory. Journal of Experimental Psychology: Learning, Memory, and Cognition, 18, 151-156. 248
- Magnussen, S., & Greenlee, M. W. (1997). Competition and sharing of processing resources in visual discrimination. Journal of Experimental Psychology: Human Perception and Performance, 23(6), 1603-1616.
- Magnussen, S., & Greenlee, M. W. (1999). The psychophysics of perceptual memory. Psychological Research, 62(2-3), 81-92.
- Magnussen, S., Greenlee, M. W., Asplund, R., & Dyrnes, S. (1991). Stimulus-specific mechanisms of visual short-term memory. Vision Research, 31 (7-8), 1213-1219.
- Magnussen, S., Greenlee, M. W., & Thomas, J. P. (1996). Parallel processing in visual short-term memory. Journal of Experimental Psychology: Human Perception and Performance, 22(1), 202-212.
- Magnussen, S., Idas, E., & Myhre, S. H. (1998). Representation of orientation and spatial frequency in perception and memory: A choice reaction time analysis. Journal of Experimental Psychology: Human Perception and Performance, 24, 707-718.

- Nilsson, T. H., & Nelson, T. M. (1981). Delayed monochromatic hue matches indicate characteristics of visual memory. Journal of Experimental Psychology: Human Perception and Performance, 7, 141-150.
- Palmer, J. (1990). Attentional limits on the perception and memory of visual information. Journal of Experimental Psychology: Human Perception and Performance, 16(2), 332-350.
- Pashler, H. (1988). Familiarity and visual change detection. Perception & Psychophysics, 44(4), 369-378.
- Pease, Alan July 1, 1984, author of Signals
- Phillips, W. A. (1974). On the distinction between sensory storage and short-term visual memory. Perception & Psychophysics, 16(2), 283-290
  Memory Skills; www.cls.utk.edu/pdf/ls/Week3_Lesson19.pdfDavid B. Ellis, *Becoming a Master Student*, College Survival Inc., Rapid City, Michigan, 1991
  *Newsweek* article, June 15, 1998, Dr. Barry Gordon and A. Sunderland, et al.
- Phillips, W. A., & Baddeley, A. D. (1971). Reaction time and short-term visual memory. Psychonomic Science, 22(2), 73-74
- Klingberg, Torkel, Oxford University Press 2009; "The Overflowing Brain"...
- Ian Parker in *The New Yorker* magazine
- The Microsoft Office Personal Productivity Challenge (PPC) March 2005
- Heinz Tschabitscher, Abbot.com Guide

- Chuvagroup.com/to-communicate-your-message-clearly  March 2011
- Robert Gunning, author of The Technique of Clear Writing
- Dave Paradi, MBA, author of "The Visual Slide Revolution" and "102 Tips to Communicate More Effectively Using PowerPoint"
- The Radicati Group, Inc. 2010 Email Statistics Report
- INC. com, March 2, 2011
- wiki.answers.com/Q/What_is_the_Average_ number_of_ words_spoken
- Neuroreport: 11 June 2003 - Volume 14 - Issue 8 - pp 1129-1133, Cognitive Neuroscience and Neuropsychology
- http://www.ncbi.nlm.nih.gov/pubmed/11515286 The magical number 4 in short-term memory: a reconsideration of mental storage capacity
- Jenkins and Dallenback's Learning Curve, http://frank.itlab.us/forgetting/mtsu_forgetting/
- Elizabeth Hilton, Differences in Visual and Auditory Short-Term Memory
- www.human-memory.net/processes_encoding. html
- Visual Short Term Working Memory, Intermediate visual store, http://en.wikipedia.org/wiki/Visual_short-term_memory
- Brain Memory2 - California Association of Independent Schools; www.caisca.org/event_info/115/Brain Memory2.doc
- Arousal-Biased Competition in Perception and Memory

Mara Mather and Matthew R. Sutherland, Department of Psychology, University of Southern California, Los Angeles, CA www.usc.edu/projects/matherlab/pdfs/MatherSutherlandin press.pdf

- Prahlad Gupta Word Learning and Verbal Short-Term Memory: A Computational Account; Beckman Institute for Advanced Science and Technology University of Illinois at Urbana-Champaign;Urbana, IL http://www.psychology.uiowa.edu/faculty/gupta/pdf/gupta.cogsci96.pdf

- The Capacity of visual Short Term Memory; www.urop.uci.edu/SURP/.../SURP%20Social%20Sciences%204.pdf

- Tech Firm Implements Employee "Zero eMail" Policy
  http://abcnews.go.com/blogs/business/2011/11/tech-company-implements-employee-zero-email-policy/

- Zefran Cochran, When Jack Welch was Deputy Director of Intelligence; https://www.cia.gov/library/center-for-the-study-of-intelligence/csi-publications/csi-studies/studies/vol48no3/article04.html

- *Franklin P. Jones Quotes* - BrainyQuote
  www.brainyquote.com/quotes/authors/f/franklin_p_jones.html

- Robert McCloskey Quotes; Thinkexist.com

- Words Per Minute FAQS http://www.turboread.com/wP.M._faqs.htm

- Zoom International; Mind your language! Monitor, evaluate, improve!; www.zoomint.com
- http://bluecentauri.com/tools/writer/sample.php
- CM150 Listening: Our Most Used Communications Skill; extension.missouri.edu/Communications
- Baddely, Alan. "Memory," Science and Technology, vol. 10, pg. 674-675
- Baddely, Alan. Your Memory: a Users Guide, United Kingdom: Prion, 1993